Who Is
Alexandria
Ocasio-Cortez?

Who Is Alexandria Ocasio-Cortez?

by Kirsten Anderson

illustrated by Manuel Gutierrez

Penguin Workshop

PENGUIN WORKSHOP
An Imprint of Penguin Random House LLC, New York

Copyright © 2021 by Penguin Random House LLC. All rights reserved.
Published by Penguin Workshop, an imprint of Penguin Random House LLC, New York.
PENGUIN and PENGUIN WORKSHOP are trademarks of Penguin Books Ltd.
WHO HQ & Design is a registered trademark of Penguin Random House LLC.
Printed in the USA.

Visit us online at www.penguinrandomhouse.com.

Library of Congress Cataloging-in-Publication Data is available upon request.

ISBN 9780593226407 (paperback)   10 9 8 7 6 5 4 3 2 1
ISBN 9780593226414 (library binding)   10 9 8 7 6 5 4 3 2 1

Contents

Who Is Alexandria Ocasio-Cortez?

Alexandria Ocasio-Cortez seemed like an unlikely candidate to take on Joseph Crowley, one of the most powerful Democrats in New York City and in Congress. But the twenty-eight-year-old bartender from the Bronx wanted to make a difference. She passionately believed that everyone should have health care and that climate change was the most urgent fight of our time.

She had walked the neighborhoods of Queens and the Bronx, trying to convince people that it was time for a change. She believed that it was time for their neighborhoods to be represented by someone who actually lived in their district, not in Washington, DC, and that it was time for them to be represented by someone who was more like them. She knew what it was like to work hard all day, as she had at restaurants in Manhattan. Alexandria—Alex to her friends—was a young, working-class Latina from one of the most ethnically diverse areas of New York City.

On the night of June 26, 2018, Alex wasn't expected to win the primary election. Most people thought she didn't have a chance. At one of their debates, Crowley had even congratulated her for bringing in "new energy" to the race, as if the result had already been decided. No one had even bothered to run against Representative Crowley for the last fourteen years. And now it was almost 9:00 p.m. The voting had ended. Alex got into the back seat of a car and prepared to watch her campaign for a seat in the US House of Representatives come to an end.

Alex's boyfriend, Riley Roberts, parked the car.

They started walking toward the campaign party. Win or lose, most campaign workers gather on the night of an election to wait out the results and celebrate, even if it's just their own hard work they are cheering for. As they passed by some large windows in the pool hall where the party was being held, Alex caught sight of TVs playing the news. She screamed and ran to the front door.

The security guard there tried to stop her. Alex pointed to a campaign poster and cried, "It's me! It's me! That's me on the poster!"

He stepped aside, and she rushed in.

The crowd roared and cheered. Alex gasped and put her hand to her mouth as she looked up at the screens. A TV reporter put a microphone in front of her, asking if she could put into words how she felt right then.

Alex paused for a moment, then said, "Nope. I cannot put this into words."

She had won.

Alexandria Ocasio-Cortez, a young Puerto Rican woman from the Bronx, had defeated Joseph Crowley. She was on her way to Congress.

CHAPTER 1
The Bronx to Yorktown

Alexandria Ocasio-Cortez was born on October 13, 1989, in the Parkchester neighborhood of the Bronx. The Bronx is one of the five boroughs that make up New York City, along with Brooklyn, Manhattan, Queens, and Staten Island. The Bronx is the only borough in New York City that has a majority Hispanic population. Alex's father, Sergio, had been born and raised in the Bronx. His family was Puerto Rican. Sergio became an architect. Her mother, Blanca, had grown up in Puerto Rico.

The Bronx was filled with family and friends, but Alex's parents were worried. In the 1990s, crime and poverty levels were higher in the Bronx than in other parts of New York City.

Sergio wanted to give Alex and her younger brother, Gabriel, a chance to get a better education. Family members helped them pull together enough money to buy a small house in Yorktown, a suburb outside of New York City.

Yorktown was different from the Bronx. Most families lived in houses, not apartments. People traveled in cars, not on subways. Most people were wealthier than Alex's family. The population was mostly white. There were very few other Latino families. At school, Alex felt no one else looked like her.

On weekends, Alex, her parents, and her brother would often go back to the Bronx to visit family. The trip between the Bronx and Yorktown was only forty minutes, but the two places seemed like different worlds. Alex began to think about how much a person's life was affected by where they were born. Some towns had wonderful public schools. A town right next door might have schools that were much worse, depending on how wealthy—or poor—the residents might be.

Alex fell in love with science when she was young. She began to dream of becoming a doctor and asked for a microscope for her birthday one year. She thought of herself as kind of a nerd. She loved the Harry Potter book series and the *Star Trek* television show.

When she was a senior in high school, Alex competed in the Intel International Science and Engineering Fair (ISEF), which attracts top high-school science students from around the world. She won second place in microbiology! To honor her work, the scientists at MIT's Lincoln Laboratory named an asteroid after her: Asteroid 23238 Ocasio-Cortez.

CHAPTER 2
Boston

Alex graduated from Yorktown High School in 2007. She had been accepted at Boston University, where she planned to study medicine. But the excitement of going to college in the fall was overshadowed by sad news: Her father had been diagnosed with cancer. Before the beginning of her sophomore year, he was hospitalized. Alex went to visit him before she left for Boston. As they talked, she began to feel like this might be the last time she saw him. When it was time for her to go, he called out to her, "Make me proud!"

Alex's father died soon after. She was crushed. Her father, she later said, "knew my soul better than anyone else on this planet."

High-school graduation, 2007

When Alex returned to Boston University, she was determined to make her father proud. She led the school's Alianza Latina (Latino/a Alliance)— a community that celebrates Latino/a culture on campus. And she began to organize meetings where students from different colleges and universities could come together and talk about issues important to them, like student-loan debt. Many students borrow money—student loans— to attend college. These loans are debt that is owed after graduation. A lot of students who were Alex's age worried they would have a hard time finding jobs when they graduated. How would they pay their debts?

From 2008 through 2009, Alex worked as an intern at the immigration and foreign affairs office of Massachusetts senator Ted Kennedy. She was the only person in the office who spoke Spanish. Many of the Spanish-speaking callers were undocumented immigrants. They were facing housing and employment troubles and needed help. Alex felt that the US government was not doing enough for them. Many simply needed documentation—proper paperwork to live and work in the United States.

During her junior year, Alex traveled to Western Africa and studied in the country of Niger. She worked at a maternity clinic. Alex was troubled by what she saw there. She watched women struggle through difficult pregnancies and saw babies die. In a wealthier country like the United States, many of their deaths could have been prevented. Once again, Alex was reminded of how different a person's life could be depending on where they happened to be born. She saw that health and wealth were closely linked.

When Alex returned to Boston, she decided that it was no longer enough to become a doctor. As a doctor, she could help only one person at a time. She switched to a double major of international relations and economics, focusing on public policy. She wanted to work on changing laws and developing programs that would help many people.

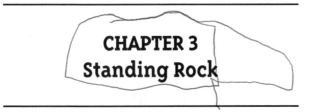

CHAPTER 3
Standing Rock

In 2011, Alex graduated with honors from Boston University. However, she also graduated with thousands of dollars in student-loan debt. Her family was struggling with their own debt after the death of her father. They were in danger of losing their Yorktown house.

Alex started working as an educational director with the National Hispanic Institute. But she had to pay rent on her apartment in the Bronx. She also had to pay student-loan bills each month, her health insurance, and she wanted to contribute to her family's expenses. Her job didn't pay enough for all that.

Alex began to wait tables at a well-known restaurant called Coffee Shop in Manhattan.

She also bartended at a taco restaurant next door called Flats Fix. Working in the restaurant business was hard. She was on her feet for hours at a time. Customers could be difficult and impatient, but she had to serve them with a smile. Tips were an important part of her salary. And she learned to listen. Sometimes people just wanted to be heard.

Other people were in the same position as Alex. They held multiple jobs as they struggled to pay off student loans. They didn't have health insurance. They were trying to keep up with their rent or hold on to their houses. The American dream of having a good-paying job and a house seemed out of reach for many people. The system seemed to be broken.

In 2016, Vermont senator Bernie Sanders campaigned to become the Democratic presidential nominee. Sanders said that everyone should be able to afford health care. He talked about making public colleges free to everyone. He believed that working-class people should be able to live dignified lives without being buried in debt. Sanders felt there was too big a gap between the country's small group of extremely wealthy people and the many who were struggling. The US government, Sanders argued, needed to make changes to narrow that gap.

Some people thought that Senator Sanders wanted a socialist government. Socialism is a form of governing where the government owns big companies. Socialist governments also often include programs like health care for all and free college. Many people believe that is what the government *should* do: take care of its

Senator Bernie Sanders

people. But many others fear socialism. They believe a socialist government might take away their personal rights.

Alex agreed with Bernie Sanders on these issues and joined his campaign. She knocked on doors in the Bronx and Queens. She found the campaign inspiring.

Senator Sanders didn't win the nomination. Former First Lady and Secretary of State Hillary Clinton became the Democratic nominee for president in 2016. In November, she lost to Republican nominee Donald J. Trump. Alex didn't think the Republican winner held any of the beliefs she felt were so important to the country.

After the election, Alex wanted to do something. There was a protest going on in North Dakota at the Standing Rock Reservation. An oil company wanted to build a pipeline that would run near the reservation. Members

of the Standing Rock Sioux tribe feared that construction of the pipeline could poison their water supply. It also could damage ancient burial grounds. They began to protest the pipeline's construction.

People from around the country traveled to Standing Rock. They joined the tribe's protest. Alex and a few friends felt that they should go, too. They set up a GoFundMe campaign to raise enough money for the trip.

The group set off from New York City. Alex livestreamed parts of their trip to her Facebook page. The videos showed her and her friends making jokes and having fun. But they also showed them having long conversations about important issues.

On the drive to Standing Rock, they made a side trip to Flint, Michigan. Flint had been in the news after reports revealed that its water supply had been poisoned by inexpensive pipes.

Protesters against oil pipelines
at Standing Rock Reservation, North Dakota

The pipes actually leaked lead into the water! People in the area began to suffer from lead poisoning. Many children would suffer lifelong damage from drinking the poisoned water. The most affected group was lower-income people of color.

Alex and her friends listened to their stories. The Flint visit made Alex think about the connections among so many of the issues she cared about. The environment, racial injustice, health, and income inequality were all linked. And she felt they could be solved together.

At Standing Rock, she was impressed by the unity and strength of the protesters. They were all working together and making an impact. She saw that anyone could have a voice and work to make a difference. She wanted to help solve the problems she saw.

But how?

The answer came more quickly than she could

have expected. On the trip back to New York City, she got a phone call from a group called Brand New Congress. They had a question for her.

Would she be interested in running for Congress?

CHAPTER 4
The Upstart

The people who had worked on the Bernie Sanders campaign saw that there was a lot of energy and interest in the progressive ideas that Sanders had campaigned on. Both Brand New Congress and Justice Democrats were groups formed by Sanders's supporters. Both wanted to help more progressive Democrats get elected to Congress. Now they just had to find the right people.

But where would they find them? Justice Democrats put a submission form on their website. They asked people to nominate candidates.

They received over ten thousand nominations! One came from Gabriel Ocasio-Cortez. He submitted his sister's name. When Brand

New Congress and Justice Democrats read about Alex, she seemed perfect. She was a young Latina, she worked in the restaurant

Alex with her brother, Gabriel

industry, and she understood how hard it was to struggle with student debt. She had worked for Sanders's campaign. Alex was comfortable with social media and able to explain her ideas clearly.

At first, Alex was unsure. She had never really considered running for office. She thought you had to be rich and powerful to get elected to Congress. People like her just didn't become congressional representatives or senators.

And that was the point Brand New Congress and Justice Democrats wanted to make. They felt that people like her *should* serve in Congress. The more she thought about it, the more sense the idea made. Alex agreed to run against Representative Joe Crowley in New York's Fourteenth Congressional District. They were both Democrats. Most of the district's voters were registered Democrats. That meant the primary winner would almost definitely defeat any Republican candidate in the November general election.

Taking on Representative Crowley was a huge task. He had been serving in Congress since 1999—almost twenty years! Many people thought he was doing a good-enough job. He even favored some progressive ideas, like a fifteen-dollar minimum wage for workers. But he didn't even live in the Bronx or Queens, the areas he represented. Crowley and his family lived in the Washington, DC, area. And he was a white man in his fifties. He had been working in politics almost his whole life. Seventy percent of the residents in the fourteenth district are people of color. Fifty percent of the district is Hispanic. Many people worked jobs where they got paid by the hour. They struggled to make ends meet. What did Crowley have in common with them?

For months, Alex and her campaign team knocked on doors to personally speak with people. They needed to get people interested in Alex and her ideas. Many people didn't answer their doors. But some listened. And Alex listened, too. Even to those who said they weren't going to vote for her. Alex wore down the soles of her shoes going door to door.

She went to farmers' markets and handed out postcards that explained why people should vote for her. She stood outside of stores and greeted shoppers. At her bartending job, she kept a paper bag full of postcards behind the counter. On breaks, she went out and handed out more postcards.

Her campaign focused on ideas that would help working-class people: a national fifteen-dollar minimum wage, health care for all, tuition-free public college and trade school, 100 percent renewable energy by 2035, and immigration reform. Alex felt that all of these issues were connected. Better pay, better health care, and a better environment would help people live better lives.

In May, Alex released a campaign video. She wrote the script and filmed it in a local bodega—a small Spanish-speaking grocery store—with her friends and family helping.

The video went viral, with over five hundred

thousand total views. It helped bring in more campaign donations. Most were small. The average donation was eighteen dollars.

But Joe Crowley's campaign was raising millions!

In June, Alex was scheduled to debate Crowley a few times. One debate was supposed to take place in the Bronx. But Crowley didn't show up. He went to a fundraiser in Queens instead. Alex was disappointed. She felt this was an insult to Bronx voters.

Alex spent Election Day out on the streets meeting people and reminding them to vote. When it was time to go to the campaign party that night, she had no idea what the voting results were. Her team had worked so hard. Still, most everyone believed Alex didn't have a chance.

But she did. On June 26, 2018, Alexandria Ocasio-Cortez won the New York Democratic primary. She was just twenty-eight years old.

CHAPTER 5
AOC

Overnight, Alex became a celebrity. She had stunned the political world with her win. The video of her shocked reaction to the news went viral. Suddenly, almost everyone knew her face and recognized her. People began to call her by just her initials: AOC.

During the summer of 2018, Alex campaigned for other progressive candidates, did interviews, and appeared on late-night talk shows. By the time she was actually elected to Congress on November 6, 2018, she was one of the most famous politicians in the United States.

Less than a week after the election, Alex joined a protest demanding action on climate change.

NOVEMBER 24 2023

She presented a plan she called the Green New
Deal. It called for Congress to form a committee
that would work to halt climate change.

Some Americans criticized the Green New

Deal. They argued that it would be too expensive or impossible to do. But many others agreed with Alex. Something had to be done about climate change, starting right away.

What's the Green New Deal?

The Green New Deal offers ideas to slow down climate change. They include:

- Switching to renewable power sources

- Building a smart energy grid that would make electricity more reliable and affordable for everyone

- Making all buildings safe, energy efficient, and water efficient

- Cutting pollution and greenhouse-gas emissions from transportation systems

- Ending the destruction of rain forests and wetlands, as well as planting trees to help offset the damage from pollution and carbon emissions

- Encouraging people to eat less meat to lower that industry's share of pollution

The Green New Deal also offers ideas for improving workers' lives and their job security, providing medical leave for workers, and strengthening labor laws.

By the time she was officially sworn in as a congresswoman on January 3, 2019, Alex had gotten used to critics. There were plenty of them. Other Democrats were jealous of her celebrity. They wondered why she got so much attention when she hadn't even done anything in her new role yet.

Republicans said her ideas weren't very logical or helpful. Some TV stations and newspapers said she was a socialist and communist who would take away everyone's private property. They warned that she wanted to raise taxes.

Alex did not let the criticism get to her. When Republicans made fun of a video showing her dancing in college, she posted a video showing her dancing into her

January 3, 2019

new congressional office.

Both Democrats and Republicans envied her success on social media. By February 2019, she had over three million Twitter followers. She also had large numbers of followers on Instagram and Facebook. Unlike most members of Congress, she had grown up with social media. She was used to livestreaming everyday moments and communicated easily with her followers. When she tweeted or wrote an Instagram post, she was using the same language as other young adults.

And she told the truth about her new life as a congresswoman. Alex pointed out that her health insurance plan as a Congress member cost less than the one she had as a bartender. That wasn't fair. She talked about how wrong it was that it was easier for her to get elected to Congress than to pay off all of her student-loan debt.

Alex was outspoken. But she also surprised other members of Congress with her willingness to listen and work with them. And she was always prepared. She worked hard to make sure she understood topics and any new issues that came up. Many people were shocked and impressed by the sharp, thoughtful questions she asked when people came to Congress to testify about different subjects.

Alex settled into life as a member of Congress. She traveled back and forth from Washington to New York to attend meetings and take questions about local issues. She and Riley got their own apartment in the Washington area. In early 2020, they got a French bulldog puppy that they named Deco. She posted videos of Deco sleeping in his carrier as she rode the train from Washington to New York.

The COVID-19 pandemic struck in early 2020, and Alex's beloved fourteenth district was one of the hardest hit areas in the United States. Hospitals in Queens were overwhelmed with sick patients. During the lockdown, Alex helped to

deliver food to people shut in their homes.

The virus underlined the issues she had been fighting for: health care for all, job

opportunities, and fixing income inequality. Many people in the United States were just barely hanging on during the best of times. An event like a pandemic could quickly turn their lives upside down.

In November 2020, Alex was reelected. She had proven herself to be more than just an interesting story. She had shown that she was a smart politician who was willing to fight for others. For many people, Alexandria Ocasio-Cortez was the face of the Democratic Party. And its best hope for the future.

Timeline of Alexandria Ocasio-Cortez's Life

1989 — Born October 13 in the Bronx, New York

1994 — Family moves to Yorktown, New York

2007 — Wins second place in microbiology in the Intel International Science and Engineering Fair

2008 — Father, Sergio Ocasio-Roman, dies

2009 — Spends semester working at a maternity clinic in Niger

2011 — Graduates from Boston University with a degree in economics and international relations

2016 — Joins the campaign for Vermont senator Bernie Sanders

— Travels to Standing Rock protest

— Asked to run for Congress in December by Brand New Congress

2017 — Officially announces congressional run in May

2018 — Quits bartending job in February

— Releases viral campaign ad on May 30

— Wins primary against US Representative Joe Crowley on June 26

2019 — Sworn into office, becoming the youngest woman ever elected to Congress

Timeline of the World

1989 — Police in Beijing, China, attack student protesters in Tiananmen Square

1990 — Tim Berners-Lee creates a model for the World Wide Web

1995 — First Sony PlayStations go on sale in the United States

1998 — Search engine Google is introduced

2001 — The first Harry Potter film, *Harry Potter and the Sorcerer's Stone*, is released

2005 — First YouTube video is uploaded

2007 — First iPhones become available

2008 — Barack Obama is elected the forty-fourth president of the United States

2012 — Superstorm Sandy strikes the East Coast of the United States

2016 — The Chicago Cubs win the World Series for the first time since 1908

2017 — First total solar eclipse to cross the continental United States since 1918 is observed

2018 — NASA probe InSight lands on Mars

2020 — Coronavirus disease COVID-19 strikes globally

Bibliography

Alter, Charlotte. " 'Change Is Closer Than We Think.' Inside Alexandria Ocasio-Cortez's Unlikely Rise." *Time*, March 21, 2019. https://time.com/longform/alexandria-ocasio-cortez-profile/.

Alter, Charlotte. *The Ones We've Been Waiting For: How a New Generation of Leaders Will Transform America*. New York: Viking, 2020.

Benwell, Max. "How Alexandria Ocasio-Cortez beat everyone at Twitter in nine tweets." *Guardian*, February 12, 2019. https://www.theguardian.com/us-news/2019/feb/12/alexandria-ocasio-cortez-twitter-social-media.

Cadigan, Hilary. "Alexandria Ocasio-Cortez Learned Her Most Important Lessons from Restaurants." *Bon Appetit*, November 7, 2018. https://www.bonappetit.com/story/alexandria-ocasio-cortez-lessons-from-restaurants.

Goldmacher, Shane. "An Upset in the Making: Why Joe Crowley Never Saw Defeat Coming." *New York Times*, June 27, 2018. https://www.nytimes.com/2018/06/27/nyregion/ocasio-cortez-crowley-primary-upset.html.

King, Georgia Frances. "Alexandria Ocasio-Cortez won a prestigious science-fair prize for research involving free radicals." *Quartz*, December 1, 2018. https://qz.com/1481551/alexandria-ocasio-cortez-won-a-2007-isef-science-fair-prize-for-her-microbiology-research/.

Lears, Rachel, dir. *Knock Down the House*. Artemis Rising
    Productions, Atlas Films, Jubilee Films, 2019. Netflix. https://
    www.netflix.com/title/81080637.

Lipsitz, Raina. "Alexandria Ocasio-Cortez Fights the Power."
    Nation, June 22, 2018. https://www.thenation.com/article/
    archive/alexandria-ocasio-cortez-fights-power/.

Murphy, Patricia. "As Alexandria Ocasio-Cortez flies high, eyes are
    rolling on the ground." *Roll Call*, January 8, 2019. https://
    www.rollcall.com/2019/01/08/as-alexandria-ocasio-cortez-
    flies-high-eyes-are-rolling-on-the-ground/.

Relman, Eliza. "The Truth About Alexandria Ocasio-Cortez: The
    inside story of how, in just one year, Sandy the bartender
    became a lawmaker who triggers both parties." *Insider*,
    January 6, 2019. https://www.insider.com/alexandria-ocasio-
    cortez-biography-2019-1.

Remnick, David. "Alexandria Ocasio-Cortez's Historic Win and
    the Future of the Democratic Party." *New Yorker*, July 16,
    2018. https://www.newyorker.com/magazine/2018/07/23/
    alexandria-ocasio-cortezs-historic-win-and-the-future-of-
    the-democratic-party.